The Ultimate Lean and Green Diet

The Best Lean and Green Cookbook for You, with 50 Easy-to-Follow Homemade Meals Recipes

By

Spoons of Happiness

Table of Contents

Introduction

For any diet or eating plan to be effective for weight loss, it is important to combine important factors such as a balanced diet, regular moderate physical exercise, and control of emotional factors such as stress and anxiety. In the case of the Lean and Green Diet, it can be stated that these factors are combined as follows:

1. It is a low-calorie and low-carbohydrate diet, due to the fact that it combines the consumption of prefabricated foods with home-prepared meals consisting mostly of lean meat or green vegetables.

2. It is recommended that people complement their diet with moderate exercise, for at least 30 minutes.

3. You can count on the support of a health coach who will motivate you and provide you with the best health and nutrition advice.

The Lean and Green diet, as mentioned above, is a low carbohydrate diet. This means that it is designed to reduce the consumption of carbohydrates, such as those found in grains, starchy vegetables and fruits, and concentrates on the consumption of those foods that are high in protein and fat. Although these types of diets are very varied in terms of the amount of calories and carbohydrates, in the particular case of the Lean and Green diet, the aim is to consume between 80 to 100 grams of carbohydrates and approximately 1000 calories.

Now, it is important to highlight the benefit of a low carbohydrate diet:

- Slimming: It is one of the main advantages or benefits of this type of diet, by reducing the amount of calories consumed and combining them with physical exercise, you begin to lose weight by increasing the amount of calories burned compared to those consumed.

- Prevention of chronic diseases or diseases associated with obesity, including diabetes, metabolic syndrome, high blood pressure and some cardiovascular diseases, by lowering or maintaining a healthy weight, and promoting healthier eating.
- Improving the level of cholesterol or blood sugar, while dieting, which can have a great impact on improving our overall health and even reversing symptoms of some diseases.
- By consuming less carbohydrates, we can improve cholesterol and triglyceride values, by consuming more lean proteins, such as fish, poultry, legumes, and green vegetables and fruits that regulate the body's functions.

In short, it is important to give yourself the opportunity to improve your health and eating habits. So let's start together on the road to weight loss with the Lean and Green diet!

Chapter 1: Snacks Recipes

In this chapter, we are going to give you some delicious and mouthwatering recipes on Octavia Snacks recipes.

1. Alabama Fire Crackers

(Ready in 2-3 Hours, Serve 30, Difficulty: Normal)

Nutrition per Serving:

Calories 218, Protein 1.2 g, Carbohydrates 12.5 g, Fat 13.9 g, Cholesterol 0mg, Sodium 320.2mg.

Ingredients:

- 1 ⅔ cup of vegetable oil

- 1 teaspoon of garlic powder

- 1 teaspoon of onion powder

- ½ teaspoon of black pepper

- 2(1 ounce) envelopes of ranch dressing mix

- 3 tablespoons of crushed red pepper flakes

- 1(16.5 ounces) package of multigrain saltine crackers

Instructions:

1. In a 2-gallon plastic zipper container, place the vegetable oil, garlic powder, black pepper, onion powder, ranch dressing blend, and crushed red pepper flakes.

2. To mix the oil and spices thoroughly, close the bag and smooch between your hands. To cover the crackers with the spice blend, put the crackers in the bag, seal, and turn it over.

3. Let the bag sit for 1 hour or so, then turn it over again. Repeat some more times and allow the bag to sit overnight till the crackers are well-coated with the spice mix.

4. Remove and serve the crackers.

2. Home-style Potato Chips

(Ready in 40 Minutes, Serve 8, Difficulty: Normal)

Nutrition per Serving:

Calories 179, Protein 2.2 g, Carbohydrates 18.6 g, Fat 11.1 g, Cholesterol 0mg, Sodium 2622.6mg.

Ingredients:

- 4 medium potatoes, peeled and paper-thin sliced

- 3 tablespoons of salt

For Deep Frying:

- 1 quart of oil

Instructions:

1. When you slice, put the potato slices into a large bowl of cold water. Drain and clean, then wash the bowl again and add the salt.

2. For at least 30 minutes, let the potatoes soak in the saline water. Drain, then rinse again and drain.

3. Heat the oil to 365 degrees Fahrenheit (185 degrees Celsius). in a deep-fryer

4. In small batches, fry the potato slices. Remove and drain on paper towels when they start turning golden. Continue until all the slices are fried.

5. If needed, season with additional salt.

3. Parmesan Thyme Crisps

(Ready in 30 Minutes, Serve 1, Difficulty: Normal)

Nutrition per Serving:

Calories 216, Protein 5.8 g, Carbohydrates 0.7 g, Fat 4.3 g, Cholesterol 13.3mg, Sodium 231.2mg.

Ingredients:

- 8 ounces of fresh-grated parmesan cheese

- 4 teaspoons of fresh thyme leaves

Instructions:

1. Preheat the oven to 300 degrees Fahrenheit (150 degrees Celsius). Line 2 parchment paper baking sheets.

2. In a bowl, mix the parmesan cheese with the thyme leaves. Into the lined baking sheets, drop heaping teaspoonfuls of the mixture, spacing them 2 inches apart. To compress them into 2-inch circles, press lightly with your fingertips.

3. Bake in the preheated oven for 8-10 minutes, until well browned and crispy. Cool slowly, around 2 minutes, on the baking sheets. With a spatula, loosen the edges and cut the parchment paper.

4. Move to wire racks and let cool completely, around 10 minutes, until firm.

4. Annie's Fruit Salsa and Cinnamon Chips

(Ready in 25 Minutes, Serve 10, Difficulty: Normal)

Nutrition per Serving:

Calories 131, Protein 6.8 g, Carbohydrates 59 g, Fat 5.9 g, Cholesterol 0mg, Sodium 461.7mg.

Ingredients:

- 2 kiwis, peeled and diced

- 2 Golden Delicious apples, peeled, cored, and diced

- 8 ounces of raspberries

- 453 g of strawberries

- 2 tablespoons of white sugar

- 1 tablespoon of brown sugar

- 3 tablespoons of fruit preserves, any flavor

- 10(10 inches) flour tortillas

- Butter flavored cooking spray

- 2 tablespoons of cinnamon sugar

Instructions:

1. In a large bowl, combine the kiwis, golden sweet apples, raspberries, bananas, white sugar, brown sugar, and fruit preserves deeply. Cover and chill for at least 15 minutes in the refrigerator.

2. Preheat the oven to 350 degrees Fahrenheit (176 degrees Celsius).

3. Coat one side of each flour tortilla with a cooking spray flavored with butter. Cut into wedges and arrange on a wide baking sheet in one single layer.

4. Sprinkle the wedges with the quantity of cinnamon sugar desired. Spray again with cooking spray.

5. Bake for 8-10 minutes in a preheated oven. Repeat for any tortilla wedges that remain. Allow it to cool for about 15 minutes.

6. Serve with a mixture of chilled fruit.

5. Salt and Pepper Skillet Fries

(Ready in 25 Minutes, Serve 6, Difficulty: Normal)

Nutrition per Serving:

Calories 128, Protein 5.6 g, Carbohydrates 48.4 g, Fat 8 g, Cholesterol 2.7mg, Sodium 134mg.

Ingredients:

- 2 tablespoons of olive oil

- 1 teaspoon of butter

- 3 large potatoes, sliced lengthwise into 1/2-inch circles and cut into 1/2-inch strips

- ¼ teaspoon of coarse sea salt

- ¼ teaspoon of cracked black pepper

Instructions:

1. Heat the olive oil and butter over medium heat in a skillet. In the hot oil-butter, cook and mix the potato strips until browned on all sides, for about 20-25 minutes.

2. Move the fries to a plate lined with paper towels and season with salt and pepper.

Chapter 2: Breakfast Recipes

In this chapter, we are going to give you some delicious and mouthwatering recipes on Octavia Breakfast recipes.

1. Baked Eggs Brunch

(Ready in 40 Minutes, Serve 4, Difficulty: Normal)

Nutrition per Serving:

Calories 210, Protein 12 g, Carbohydrates 10 g, Fat 13 g, Saturates 3 g, Sugars 7 g, Fiber 5 g, Salt 0.5 g.

Ingredients:

- 2 tablespoons of olive oil

- 2 leeks, thinly sliced

- 2 onions, thinly sliced

- 2 (100 g each) bags of baby spinach leaves

- Handful fresh wholemeal breadcrumbs

- 25 g of finely grated parmesan (or vegetarian alternative)

- 4 heat dried tomatoes, chopped

- 4 medium eggs

Instructions:

1. Heat oven to 200 degrees Celsius (392 F)/fan 180 degrees Celsius/gas 6. In a skillet, heat the oil and combine the leeks, onions, and seasoning it.

2. Cook until smooth and begin to caramelize for 15-20 minutes.

3. Meanwhile, place the spinach in a colander and pour a hot water kettle over it. Squeeze out as much liquid as possible while it is cold enough to handle. Mix the breadcrumbs and butter.

4. Arrange the leek and onion mixture between 4 ovenproof bowls, then scatter with the spinach and the sliced tomato. In the center of each dish, make a well and crack an egg in it. Season with the cheese crumbs and sprinkle.

5 Place the dishes on a baking tray and cook for 12-15 minutes until the whites are fixed and the yolks are cooked to your preference.

2. Creamy Yogurt Porridge

(Ready in 10 Minutes, Serve 6, Difficulty: Easy)

Nutrition per Serving:

Calories 184, Protein 13 g, Carbohydrates 26 g, Fat 2 g, Saturates 0 g, Sugars 13 g, Fiber 3 g, Salt 0.4 g.

Ingredients:

- 3 tablespoons(25 g) of porridge oat

- 1 pot (150 g) of 0% fat probiotic yogurt

Instructions:

1. In a shallow non-stick cup, combine 200ml of water and mix in the porridge oats.

2. Cook over low heat until bubbling and thickened. (To make in a microwave, use a deep container to prevent

spillage as the mixture will rise as it cooks, and cook for 3 minutes on high.)

3. Stir in yogurt, or swirl in 1/2 and top with the rest.

4. Serve plain or with 1 of our toppings.

3. Spicy Moroccan Eggs

(Ready in 40 Minutes, Serve 4, Difficulty: Normal)

Nutrition per Serving:

Calories 269, Protein 16 g, Carbohydrates 22 g, Fat 10 g, Saturates 2 g, Sugars 11 g, Fiber 8 g, Salt 1 g.

Ingredients:

- 2 teaspoons of rapeseed oil

- 1 large onion, halved and thinly sliced

- 3 cloves of garlic, sliced

- 1 tablespoon of rose harissa

- 1 teaspoon of ground coriander

- 150ml of vegetable stock

- 400 g of can chickpea

- 2 (400 g) cans of cherry tomatoes

- 2 courgettes, finely diced

- 200 g bag baby spinach

- 4 tablespoons of chopped coriander

- 4 large eggs

Instructions:

1. In a big deep-frying pan, heat the oil and fry the onion and garlic for around 8 minutes, stirring from time to time, until the onion and garlic turn golden.

2. Add the harissa and ground coriander, mix well and then dump the liquid into the stock and chickpeas.

3. To thicken the stock a bit, cover and boil for 5 minutes, then mash around one-third of the chickpeas.

4. Put the tomatoes and courgettes in the pan and cook gently until the courgettes are soft, for 10 minutes. Fold the spinach into the pan such that it wilts.

5. In the mixture, stir in the minced cilantro, make 4 hollows, and split into the shells.

6. Cover and cook for 2 minutes, then take off the heat and allow 2 minutes before serving to settle.

4. Fig, Nut & Seed Bread with Ricotta & Fruit

(Ready in 2 Hours and 45 Minutes, Serve 16, and Difficulty: Normal)

Nutrition per Serving:

Calories 249, Protein 10 g, Carbohydrates 30 g, Fat 10 g, Saturates 3 g, Sugars 20 g, Fiber 6 g, Salt 0.3 g.

Ingredients:

- 400ml of hot strong black tea

- 100 g of dried fig, hard stalks removed, thinly sliced

- 140 g of sultana scones

- 50 g of porridge oat

- 200 g of self-raising whole meal flour

- 1 teaspoon of baking powder

- 100 g of mixed nuts (almonds, walnuts, Brazils, hazelnuts)

- 1 tablespoon of golden linseed

- 1 tablespoon of sesame seeds, plus 2 teaspoons to sprinkle

- 25 g of pumpkin seed

- 1 large egg

- 25 g of ricotta per person

- 1 orange or green apple, thickly sliced, per person

For Topping:

- 50 g of mixed nuts

Instructions:

1. Heat oven to 170 degrees Celsius(338 F)/fan 150 degrees Celsius/gas 3½. Pour the tea into a large bowl and stir in the figs, sultanas, and oats. Set aside to soak.

2. Meanwhile, line 1 kg loaf tin with baking parchment on the base and bottom.

3. Mix the rice, baking soda, nuts, and seeds. In the cooled fruit mixture, beat the egg and then stir the dried ingredients into the liquid one. With the additional nuts and sesame seeds, dump into the tin, then level the surface and disperse.

4. Bake for 1 hour, then cover the top with foil and bake until a skewer inserted into the loaf center comes out clean for 15 more minutes.

5. To cool, remove from the tin but keep the parchment on until cold. Spread with ricotta, split into pieces, and serve with berries.

6. Store in the refrigerator for one month, or freeze into slices.

5. Baked Salmon & Eggs

(Ready in 20 Minutes, Serve 6, Difficulty: Normal)

Nutrition per Servings:

Calories 238, Protein 15 g, Carbohydrates 22 g, Fat 10 g, Saturates 4 g, Sugars 1 g, Fiber 1 g, Salt 2 g.

Ingredients:

- 6 crusty white rolls

- 25 g of melted butter

- 6 slices of smoked salmon gravlax

- 6 medium eggs

- A few snipped of chives

Instructions:

1. Heat oven to 180 degrees Celsius (356 F)/fan 160 degrees Celsius/gas 4.

2. Cut the top of each roll-off, then gently cut the bread's interior until an opening is wide enough to suit

a slice of salmon and an egg. Arrange the rolls on a baking dish, with the tops reserved.

2. Using a little melted butter to brush the rolls' inside and sides, arrange a salmon slice inside each. Crack each 1 with an egg and season. Bake until the eggs are cooked to your taste or for 10-15 minutes. With snipped chives, disperse.

3. Brush the tops with the remaining butter, split them into troops, and dip them into shells.

Chapter 3: Lunch Recipes

In this chapter, we are going to give you some delicious and mouthwatering recipes on Octavia Lunch recipes.

1. Low-Calorie Microwave Dhokla (Indian Recipe)

(Ready in 30 Minutes, Serve 6, Difficulty: Easy)

Nutrition per Serving:

Calories 267, Protein 10.2 g, Carbohydrates 34.4 g, Fat 9.8 g, Sugars 2.6 g.

Ingredients:

- 1 cup of besan 1 tsp suji

- 1 teaspoon of ginger, green chili paste

- 1 teaspoon of salt

- 1/2 lemon, juiced

- 1 teaspoon of turmeric powder

- 2 tablespoons of. curd

- 1 cup of water

- 1 teaspoon of fruit salt

For Tadka:

- 2 teaspoon of oil

- 1 teaspoon of mustard seeds

- 15-20 curry leaves

- 2 green chilies

- 1 teaspoon of sesame seeds

- 1 cup of water

For Garnish:

- Coriander leaves

- Grated coconut

Instructions:

1. In a big deep bowl, take besan. Use green chili paste to add suji and ginger to it.

2. Thoroughly mix them, add salt and lemon juice, and mix again. Add the turmeric powder and curd and thoroughly whisk.

3. Pour some water in the bowl and whisk thoroughly to make a thick batter of the put fruit salt in the batter and mix.

4. Transfer the batter for 6-8 minutes to a microwave-friendly utensil and heat it on high power.

5. Put the mustard seeds in a hot oil pan and prepare the tadka. Cook the curry leaves and green chilies a little, then add them to the tadka and cook thoroughly. Add the sesame seeds and some water to balance them well.

4.Pour the tadka over cooked dhokla. Garnish with grated coconut and coriander leaves.

5. Slice the dish into the appropriate sizes and serve it fresh.

2. Matcha Tea Macaroons

(Ready in 1 Hour and 15 Minutes, Serve 12, Difficulty: Normal)

Nutrition per Serving:

Calories 127, Protein 2 g, Carbohydrates 18 g, Fat 5 g, Fiber 0 g, Sugar 17 g.

Ingredients:

For Macaroons:

- 5 egg whites

- 20 g of breakfast sugar

- 368 g of icing sugar

- 425 g of almond powder

- 1 tablespoon of matcha powder

For White Chocolate Ganache:

- 60ml of heavy cream

- 170 g of chopped white chocolate

Instructions:

Prepare Macaroon Shells:

1. Place and set aside 2 silicone mats on 2 wide baking trays.

2. Mix the almond flour, icing sugar, and matcha powder well. Set aside.

3. Whip the egg whites at a medium-low speed using an electric mixer until they are frothy. Sprinkle the granulated sugar slowly and continue to whip until it forms stiff peaks.

4. To fit the remaining materials, move the egg whites to a wide bowl.

5. Fold ¼ of the blend of almond flour gently into the whites. Fold in the remaining almond mixture gradually until a moist, gloppy batter forms. It needs to have hot lava consistency.

6. Rapidly fill the batter with a pastry bag, or the meringue may loosen. Pipe into 2-inch rounds, spaced about 1-inch apart, onto the prepared baking sheets.

7. Let the macarons rest at room temperature for 25-40 minutes, until the tops are dry and smooth skin has formed.

8. Adjust the oven rack to the middle position for 10 minutes before baking and heat the oven to 160 degrees Celsius (320 F).

9. Bake on the one hand for 6 minutes, turn the tray around and bake for another 6 minutes. At a time, bake one pan.

10. Slide the silicone mat carefully onto a wire rack or the marble tabletop immediately after baking, and cool completely.

Prepare White Chocolate Ganache:

1. Put it to a boil with the milk. Pour over the white diced chocolate and mix to an even consistency. Using a spatula made of wood and not a machine. Leave to cool at room temperature to thicken more.

2. Pour into a piping bag once thick enough to pipe, pipe gently onto one macaroon shell, and put the other macaron shell on top. Push a little until the ganache spreads to the sides.

3. Serve.

3. Buckwheat Blinis Sandwich with Beetroot and Feta

(Ready in 55 Minutes, Serve 4, Difficulty: Normal)

Nutrition per Serving:

Calories 229, Protein 2.7 g, Carbohydrates 5.7 g, Fat 3.2 g, Cholesterol 21.7mg, Sodium 75.5mg.

Ingredients:

- 150 gram of buckwheat flour

- ½ teaspoon of baking powder

- 2 g of salt

- 1 teaspoon of yogurt

- 1 ½ teaspoon of vinegar

- 150ml of water

- 10 gram of jalapenos

- 10ml of clarified butter

- 160 g of beetroot, chopped

- 35 g of castor sugar

- 75ml of vinegar

- ½ teaspoon of cumin powder

- ½ teaspoon of coriander powder

- 20 g of walnut

- 80 g of feta

Instructions:

1. In a medium-sized bowl, sift the buckwheat flour.

2. Add baking powder, salt, vinegar, yogurt, and blend well. Add water slowly.

3. To the mixture, add sliced jalapenos, which should have a pancake batter's consistency for 15 minutes, set aside.

4. In a non-stick pan over moderate heat, melt a little butter.

5. In the hot skillet, spoon tablespoon-size mounds of batter and cook until bubbles form on the surface and the rim, the blinis are browned.

6. Blinis is turned and cooked for 15 seconds longer.

7. Peel the beetroot and finally chop it.

8. Over low heat, melt the sugar. In the pan, add chopped beetroot, vinegar, water, cumin powder, cilantro powder and cook for 10-15 minutes, stirring frequently.

9. Add chopped walnut to the mixture, remove from the heat, and allow to cool.

10. Place each blini with 1 tablespoon of beetroot mixture and top with feta cheese.

11. Garnish and serve with a rocket leaf.

4. Quinoa and Sesame Crackers with Orange Hummus

(Ready in 50 Minutes, Serve 8, Difficulty: Normal)

Nutrition per Serving:

Calories 331, Protein 1 g, Carbohydrates 2 g, Fat 1 g, Saturated Fat 1 g, Cholesterol 8mg, Sodium 39mg.

Ingredients:

- 200 gram of white quinoa

- 500ml of water to cook quinoa

- ½ teaspoon of baking powder

- 50 gram of rice flour

- 5 gram of salt

- 15 gram of sesame seeds

- 2 fresh oranges

- 150 g of boiled chickpeas

- 20 g of tahini paste

- 2 pinches of smoked paprika

- Salt, to taste

Instructions:

1. Preheat the oven to 176 degree Celsius (350°F)

2. Bring quinoa to a boil over moderate heat, then simmer until fully cooked and consistency is achieved like porridge.

3. Remove it from the heat and let it cool down.

4. To blend, add rice flour, baking powder, season with salt and mix well.

5. Using a spatula, spread the quinoa batter on to the silpat®.

6. Sprinkle with the sesame seeds and cook for 10-12 minutes.

7. Take it out of the oven and allow it to cool.

8. Using the fine side of your grater, prepare the orange zest. When the zest has been extracted, split the orange in ½ and squeeze out the orange juice.

9. Add the boiled chickpeas, smoked paprika, orange juice, tahini paste, salt, and process until well mixed in a food processor.

10. Move the hummus and search for seasoning in a serving bowl. Serve with crackers made from quinoa. Enjoy!

5. Veg Summer Rolls

(Ready in 40 Minutes, Serve 6, Difficulty: Normal)

Nutrition per Serving:

Calories 81, Protein 3 g, Carbs 16 g, Fat 0 g, Fiber 1 g.

Ingredients:

- 2 rice paper sheets

- 25 g of iceberg lettuce

- 25 g of carrot

- 10 g of bean sprouts

- 15 g of cucumber

- 15 g of tofu

- 5 basil leaves

- 5 mint leaves

- 5 coriander leaves

- 15 g of rice noodles (soaked in warm water for 20-25 minutes)

- 5 cups of peanuts, roasted

For the Hoisin Peanut Sauce:

- 45 g of hoisin sauce

- 30 roasted peanuts

- 5 chopped garlic

- 15ml of oil

- 10 chopped red chilies

- 50ml of water

Instructions:

1. Make a paste from the peanuts roasted (Add 15ml of water and 15ml of cooking oil, grind in a mixer until a smooth paste. Add a little more water if required). Add the peanut paste, garlic, hoisin sauce, and chilies into a non-stick pan.

2. Add about 50ml of water and let it boil until the sauce thickens. Allow cooling.

3. Slice the carrot and cucumber thinly. Let the tofu sliced into batons.

4. Take a sheet of rice paper and put it for 10-15 seconds in water. Place it on a flat surface by wiping your hands with excess water.

5. Layer it with slices of cucumber and carrot, accompanied by sprouts of tofu, beans, roasted peanuts, basil leaves, iceberg lettuce, mint leaves, and coriander leaves.

6. Over it, put the rice noodles and chicken. Drizzle more sauce.

7. Roll the rice paper. Fold the sides after the first roll and roll further. To prevent the filling from dropping out, ensure that it is rolled tightly.

8. At a slant, cut the roll and serve with the hoisin peanut sauce.

9. For the second layer, repeat the procedure.

6. Semiya Upma (Indian Recipe)

(Ready in 30 Minutes, Serve 12, Difficulty: Easy)

Nutrition per Serving:

Calories 180, Protein 2.6 g, Carbohydrates 17.4 g, Fat 11.1 g, Fiber 1.5 g.

Ingredients:

- 2 tablespoons of oil

- 1 teaspoon of mustard seeds

- 1 teaspoons of cumin seeds

- 1 teaspoon of peanuts

- ½ teaspoons of sesame seeds

- 1 teaspoon of black gram

- 7-8 curry leaves

- 11-12 cashew nuts

- 1 onion, chopped

- ¼ cup of chopped carrot

- ¼ cup of chopped beans

- ¼ cup of peas

- 1 teaspoon of ginger

- 1 green chili

- 1 teaspoon of salt

- ½ teaspoon of turmeric powder

- 1 cup of vermicelli

- 1 cup of water

Instructions:

1. In a pan, heat oil.

2. Add the mustard seeds, peanuts, sesame, black gram, curry leaves, and cashew nuts.

3. For a while, cook them and add the onion and combine thoroughly.

4. Along with ginger, peas, and green chili, add chopped carrot and beans. Stir occasionally.

5. Add the salt and turmeric powder and blend until the color is yellowish.

6. Pour the vermicelli slowly into the pan.

7. Stir slowly by adding water as needed.

8. To let it cook on a medium flame, cover the pan for a while.

9. If the water has evaporated, remove the lid and check.

10. Semiya Upma is ready for a hot serving.

Chapter 4: Dinner Recipes

In this chapter, we are going to give you some delicious and mouthwatering recipes on Octavia Dinner recipes.

1. Roasted Butternut Squash and Chickpea Curry

(Ready in 55 Minutes, Serve 6, Difficulty: Normal)

Nutrition per Serving:

Calories 243, Protein 8.3 g, Fat 5.5 g, Sodium 399.7mg, Potassium ,076.7mg, Sugars 4.6 g,

Ingredients:

- 1 medium (about 3-4 cups) butternut squash, cubed

- 2 tablespoons of coconut oil

- 1 red onion

- 4 cloves of garlic

- 1 thumb-sized piece of ginger

- 1 tablespoon of curry powder

- 1 teaspoon of garam masala

- 1/2 teaspoon of ground cumin

- 1/2 teaspoon of cumin seeds

- 1/4 teaspoon of turmeric

- 1/4 teaspoon of hot chili powder

- 1 tin(400ml) of chopped tomatoes

- 1 tin(400ml) of coconut milk

- 200ml of vegetable stock

- 1 tin(400 g) of chickpeas

- Salt and pepper

To serve:

- Chopped coriander

- Basmati rice

Instructions:

1. Preheat oven to 400 degrees Fahrenheit (204 Celsius). Cut the squash from both sides, slice it and cut it lengthwise in half. Cut into cubes of approximately equal size, around 1 cm.

2. Place on a large baking tray, drizzle with salt and pepper oil, toss and place for 35-40 minutes in the oven until soft and brown on the edges.

3. In the meantime, start the curry. On medium heat, add coconut oil to a large pan, and once melted, add the finely chopped onion. For a few minutes, stir and fry, then add crushed garlic and grated ginger. Leave it for another minute to cook.

4. All the spices are added: curry powder, garam masala, and seeds of turmeric, and chili powder. Cook for 30 seconds until fragrant. If necessary, add a little more oil so that it does not burn.

5. Mix in the chopped tomatoes, coconut milk, and stock of vegetables. Simmer gently and let cook for 10 minutes. Transfer to a bowl and blend until smooth with a hand mixer or a food processor. Transfer to the pan again.

6. Add the chickpeas and cook for another 5-10 minutes. It should be thickened and sweet, creamy, and orange in color. Taste the sauce and add salt and pepper to the seasoning. You should add some additional chili powder if you like it spicy.

7. Add the butternut squash roast, stir, and serve. Top with some chopped fresh cilantro and serve with your favorite sides and basmati rice, like onion bhajis.

2. Quinoa with Broccoli Pesto

(Ready in 30 Minutes, Serve 6, Difficulty: Easy)

Nutrition per Serving:

Calories 359, Protein 12 g, Carbohydrates 16 g, Fat 23 g, Sodium 406mg, Potassium 509mg.

Ingredients:

- 1 cup of quinoa rinsed

- 2 cups of water

- 5 cups of fresh broccoli cut into small florets (about 2 good size broccoli crowns)

- 4 cloves of garlic

- 2/3 cup of freshly grated parmesan, divided

- 2/3 cup of sliced or slivered almonds toasted, divided

- 1/2 teaspoon of salt

- Juice from 1 fresh lemon (2 tablespoons)

- 1/4 cup of olive oil

- 1/4 cup of heavy cream

Optional Toppings:

- Chopped basil red Chile oil (recipe below)

- Sliced avocado

- To make this dish vegan substitute the heavy cream with coconut milk. For the parmesan cheese, you can use Parma, or add about ¼ cup of sesame seeds in place of the parmesan cheese.

Instructions:

1. Heat the quinoa with 2 cups of water in a medium saucepan until it boils. Reduce flame, cover, and simmer until all the water and quinoa fluffs are absorbed, for about 15 minutes. When the seeds have sprouted, quinoa is done. Set aside.

2. Heat a large pot of water to boiling and add the broccoli. Only cook long enough to bring out the raw taste and until the broccoli is bright green. Roughly 90 seconds. Drain the broccoli and rinse with cold water to prevent further cooking of the broccoli. Set aside.

3. Mash 2 cups of cooked broccoli, garlic, 1/3 cup of almonds, 1/3 cup of parmesan cheese, salt, and lemon juice in a food processor to make the broccoli pesto. Drizzle in the cream and olive oil and pulse until almost smooth.

4. Toss the quinoa and remaining broccoli florets with the broccoli pesto just before serving. Taste, and at this point, you might decide to add more lemon juice or salt. Add and taste the remaining 1/3 cup of parmesan cheese. When you like, add more.

5. On serving dishes or bowls, spoon the mixture. Add your chosen toppings. Sliced avocado and liberal quantities of red chili oil are strongly recommended.

Red Chile Oil:

1. In a small saucepan, heat 1/2 cup of extra-virgin olive oil until heated, but not so hot that it smokes.

2. Stir in 1 1/2 teaspoon of crushed red pepper flakes and turn off the heat.

3. Put aside and let it cool down. It is well prepared the day before and stored overnight in the refrigerator.

4. Before using it, return to room temperature again.

3. "Flush the Fat Away" Lentil and Vegetable Soup

(Ready in 45 Minutes, Serve 10, Difficulty: Normal)

Nutrition per Serving:

Calories 72, Protein 1 g, Carbohydrates 11 g, Fat 3 g, Sodium 633mg, Potassium 272mg, Fiber 3 g.

Ingredients:

- 2 cups of dry lentils rinsed

- 1 cup of dry quinoa rinsed

- 2 carrots shredded

- 1 sweet potato cut into bite-size pieces

- 1 yellow onion diced

- 2 cloves of garlic minced

- 5 cups of vegetable broth low-sodium (no sugar added)

- 4 ounces of diced green chiles

- 2 teaspoon of chili powder

- 1 teaspoon of cumin

- 1/4 teaspoon of crushed red pepper flakes

- 1 teaspoon of black pepper

- 1/2 teaspoon of sea salt (or to taste)

- 2 cups of chard torn and packed, center stem removed

- 1 avocado, chopped

- 1/2 cup of chopped fresh cilantro

Instructions:

1. In a big pot, add all the ingredients, except the last three (chard, avocado, and cilantro). Bring to a boil, reduce the heat to a low boil, cover and leave the lid slightly.

2. Cook for about 30 minutes, until the lentils and quinoa are tender.

3. Add a torn Swiss card and cook for about 5 minutes, until wilted.

4. Use diced avocado and chopped cilantro to serve and top.

4. Skinny Broccoli Cheese Soup Recipe

(Ready in 25 Minutes, Serve 6, Difficulty: Normal)

Nutrition per Serving:

Calories 200, Protein 16 g, Carbohydrates 15 g, Fat 10 g.

Ingredients:

- 1 tablespoon of butter

- 1 small yellow onion roughly chopped

- 1 stalk of celery, roughly chopped

- 2 cloves of garlic, minced

- 1 teaspoon of salt plus, (or to taste)

- 1/2 teaspoon of nutmeg

- 1/4 teaspoon of fresh pepper

- 3 1/2 cups of vegetable broth more as needed to thin out to desired consistency

- 1 cup of skim milk

- 1(16 ounces) bag of frozen cauliflower florets

- 1 medium carrot shredded

- 1(16 ounces) bag of frozen broccoli florets

- 1 1/2 (6-8 ounces) cup of reduced-fat shredded sharp cheddar

Instructions:

1. Melt butter over medium/medium-high heat in a large soup pot.

2. Add the chopped onion, celery, garlic, and spices and cook for 5 minutes or so.

3. Bring to a boil and add the broth, milk, and cauliflower.

4. Simmer until the cauliflower is tender with a fork, around 3-5 minutes.

5. To mix, use an immersion blender.

6. Add the carrots and broccoli and simmer until the broccoli, about 5 minutes, is cooked to your taste.

7. To mix, use an immersion blender.

8. Add the cheese until it is melted.

9. Re-season and taste, if necessary, and serve!

5. Healthy Spinach Lasagna Rolls

(Ready in 30 Minutes, Serve 9, Difficulty: Hard)

Nutrition per Serving:

Calories 216, Fat 15.9 g, Polyunsaturated Fat 0.4 g, Monounsaturated Fat 2.5 g, Sodium 1,188.6mg.

Ingredients:

- 9 Lasagna noodles, cooked

- 1(10 ounces) package of frozen chopped spinach thawed and completely drained

- 1(15 ounces) container of ricotta cheese

- 1/2 cup of grated parmesan cheese

- 1 egg

- 1/2 teaspoon of minced garlic

- 1/2 teaspoon of dried Italian seasonings

- Salt and fresh pepper

- 1 chicken breast cooked and diced (Optional)

- 32 ounces of marinara sauce

- 9 tablespoons of shredded, part-skim mozzarella cheese

Instructions:

1. Preheat the oven to 350 degrees Fahrenheit (176 Celsius).

2. Make sure the spinach drains well.

3. In a medium cup, mix the spinach, parmesan cheese, ricotta, egg, garlic, chicken, Italian seasonings, and salt and pepper. On the bottom of a 9x13-inch baking platter, add around 1 cup of sauce.

4. On the table, put a piece of wax paper and lay out the lasagna noodles. By patting them with a paper towel,

make sure the noodles are dry. Take 1/3 cup of the mixture of ricotta and spread it evenly on a noodle. Place seam side down on the baking dish and roll carefully. Repeat with the noodles that remain.

5. In the baking dish, ladle sauce over the noodles and top each one with 1 tablespoon of mozzarella cheese. Tightly cover the baking dish with aluminum foil and cook for 40 minutes, or until the cheese is melted. Makes nine rolls.

6. Place a little sauce on the plate to serve and top with a lasagna roll

6. Skinny Teriyaki Pork Chops with Pineapple

(Ready in 3 Hours and 10 Minutes, Serve 6, and Difficulty: Hard)

Nutrition per Serving:

Calories 201, Protein 25 g, Carbohydrates: 9.4 g, Fat 6.7 g, Saturated Fat 2.3 g, Fiber 0.5 g, Sugar 8 g.

Ingredients:

- ⅓ cup of Tropicana® Trop50® orange juice or canned pineapple juice

- 2 tablespoons of less-sodium soy sauce

- 1 tablespoon of rice vinegar

- 1 tablespoon of brown sugar

- ½ teaspoon of ground ginger

- ½ teaspoon of onion powder

- ½ teaspoon of garlic powder

- 4(4-ounces) boneless pork chops, trimmed of fat

- 2 teaspoons of corn-starch

- 4 thickly sliced fresh pineapple rings

Instructions:

1. Mix the orange juice, ground ginger, soy sauce, rice vinegar, brown sugar, onion powder, and garlic powder in a small bowl to make a marinade.

2. In a large reseal able container, place the pork chops and add the marinade to cover. Seal the bag and place

it in the refrigerator overnight for at least 2 hours. To coat the pork chops uniformly with the marinade, turn the bag every hour or so, if possible.

3. To a shallow dish, transfer the pork chops. In a small saucepan, pour the marinade into it.

4. Dissolve the corn-starch in a small bowl into 2 teaspoons of cold water to form a slurry. Place the marinade casserole over medium heat and bring it to a boil. Lower the heat to a low level and whisk in the slurry. Cook for about 2 minutes, whisking, until the sauce thickens. Remove from the heat and set aside to use as a base for the pineapple and grilled pork chops.

5. Preheat the medium-high heat of an outdoor grill, grill pan, or outdoor grill. Cover lightly with cooking spray on the grill rack of the indoor grill or grill pan.

6. Place the pork chops on the grill and cook until the inner temperature reaches 145 degrees Fahrenheit, 4-5 minutes on each side, sometimes brushing as you grill with the baste.

7. Add the pineapple slices to the grill and cook on both sides for 1-2 minutes.

8. Right before serving, let the pork chops rest for 2-4 minutes.

9. To serve, on top of each pork chop, place 1 grilled pineapple slice and serve with any remaining marinade sauce.

Chapter 5: Soups Recipes

In this chapter, we are going to give you some delicious and mouthwatering recipes on Octavia Soups recipes.

1. Spaetzle and Chicken Soup

(Ready in 2 hrs. 20 Minutes, Serve 8, and Difficulty: Hard)

Nutrition per Serving:

Calories 126, Protein 36.3 g, Carbohydrates 45.3 g, Fat 25.2 g, Cholesterol 222.7mg, Sodium 648mg.

Ingredients:

- 1(1360 g) of a whole chicken

- 2(14.5 ounces) of cans chicken broth

- 2 medium yellow onions, quartered

- 1 bunch of celery with leaves, cut into pieces

- 1(16 ounces) package of baby carrots

- Salt and ground black pepper, to taste

- ½ teaspoon of garlic salt, or to taste

- 5 eggs

- ½ cup of water

- 1 teaspoon of salt

- 3 cups of all-purpose flour

- ½ teaspoon of parsley flakes

Instructions:

1. Place the chicken and add enough water to cover it in a stockpot. Pour in the chicken broth and add the onions and celery. Add salt, pepper, and garlic salt to the seasoning. Bring it to a boil and simmer for 1 hour or so to get a healthy broth.

2. Remove it to a plate when the chicken is cooked and tender, and let sit until it is cool enough to treat. Strain the broth and discard the onions and celery. Take the broth back to the stockpot. Strip the chicken meat from the bones, slice it or break it into bits, and add it to the oven. Boil the broth and add the carrots.

3. Then stir together the eggs, water, and salt in a medium dish. Add flour gradually until the dough is firm enough for a ball to form. You can need more flour

or less. On a flat plate, pat the dough out. Cut slices of dough from the side of the plate with a butter knife until they are around 2-3 inches long. Allow them to fall straight into the broth that is boiling.

4. The soup is ready until the carrots are tender. Sprinkle with flakes of parsley and serve.

2. Thai Chicken Cabbage Soup

(Ready in 45 Minutes, Serve 6, Difficulty: Normal)

Nutrition per Serving:

Calories 227, Protein 20.8 g, Carbohydrates 42.3 g, Fat 3.1 g Cholesterol 61.3mg, Sodium 118.3mg.

Ingredients:

- 3 skinless, boneless chicken breast halves

- 8 cups of chicken broth

- 2 leeks, sliced

- 6 carrots, cut into 1-inch pieces

- 1 medium head cabbage, shredded

- 1(8 ounces) package of uncooked egg noodles

- 1 teaspoon of Thai Chile sauce

Instructions:

1. Place the chicken breasts in a stockpot or Dutch oven with the broth. Bring to a boil and simmer for 20 minutes or until the chicken is fully cooked. To cool, remove the chicken from the broth and set it aside.

2. In the pot, place the leeks and carrots and simmer for 10 minutes, or until tender. Into bite-sized bits, shred the cooled chicken and return it to the pot.

3. Add the noodles to the cabbage and egg and simmer for another 5 minutes or until the noodles are tender. Like a stew, the broth should be thick.

4. Serve hot with Thai chili sauce and season to taste.

3. Cabbage Fat-Burning Soup

(Ready in 45 Minutes, Serve 1, Difficulty: Normal)

Nutrition per Serving:

Calories 290, Protein 4 g, Carbohydrates 20.7 g, Fat 0.5 g, Cholesterol 0mg, Sodium 483.1mg.

Ingredients:

- 5 carrots, chopped

- 3 onions, chopped

- 2(16 ounces) cans of whole peeled tomatoes, with liquid

- 1 large head cabbage, chopped

- 1(1 ounce) envelope of dry onion soup mix

- 1(15 ounces) can of cut green beans, drained

- 2 quarts of tomato juice

- 2 green bell peppers, diced

- 10 stalks of celery, chopped

- 1(14 ounces) can of beef broth

Instructions:

1. Place the chicken breasts in a stockpot or Dutch oven with the broth. Bring to a boil and simmer for 20 minutes or until the chicken is fully cooked. To cool, remove the chicken from the broth and set it aside.

2. In the pot, place the leeks and carrots and simmer for 10 minutes, or until tender. Into bite-sized bits, shred the cooled chicken and return it to the pot.

3. Add the noodles to the cabbage and egg and simmer for another 5 minutes or until the noodles are tender. Like a stew, the broth should be thick.

4. Serve hot with Thai chili sauce and season to taste.

4. Portuguese Chicken Soup II

(Ready in 40 Minutes, Serve 6, Difficulty: Normal)

Nutrition per Serving:

Calories 159, Protein 16.8 g, Carbohydrates 6.8 g, Fat 7.1 g, Cholesterol 49.1mg, Sodium 63.2mg.

Ingredients:

- 1 whole bone-in chicken breast, with skin

- 1 onion, cut into thin wedges

- 4 sprigs fresh parsley

- ½ teaspoon of lemon zest

- 1 sprig fresh mint

- 6 cups of chicken stock

- ⅓ cup of thin egg noodles

- 2 tablespoons of chopped fresh mint leaves

- Salt, to taste

- ¼ teaspoon of freshly ground white pepper

Instructions:

1. Simmer the chicken breast in stock in a large saucepan with the onion, lemon zest, parsley, and mint sprig until cooked, about 35 minutes.

2. Cool, remove the breast, then peel the meat off and cut it into julienne.

3. Strain the broth, bring it back to the pot, and bring it to a boil. Pasta and chopped mint are included. Season with salt and white pepper to taste. Heat before the al dente pasta is cooked.

4. Stir in the lemon juice and chicken julienne, and remove from the heat. Ladle it into soup dishes and cover it with lemon and mint leaf pieces.

5. Classic Jewish Chicken Soup

(Ready in 4 Hours and 15 Minutes, Serve 1, and Difficulty: Hard)

Nutrition per Serving:

Calories 200, Protein 18.5 g, Carbohydrates 21.2 g, Fat 4.7 g, Cholesterol 48mg, Sodium 283.3mg.

Ingredients:

- 1 whole chicken, giblets removed

- 2 large onions, chopped

- Water to cover

- 2 tablespoons of dried dill weed (Optional)

- 2 tablespoons of dried parsley (Optional)

- Salt and ground black pepper, to taste

- 4 large carrots, peeled and cut into cubes

- 2 potatoes, peeled and cut into cubes

- 2 leeks, diced

- 3 stalks of celery, diced

- 1 large kohlrabi bulb, peeled and diced

- 3 parsnips, peeled and cut into cubes

- 2 tablespoons of chicken bouillon granules (Optional)

- Salt and ground black pepper, to taste.

Instructions:

1. Simmer the chicken breast in stock in a large saucepan with the onion, lemon zest, parsley, and mint sprig until cooked, about 35 minutes.

2. Cool, remove the breast, then peel the meat off and cut it into julienne.

3. Strain the broth, bring it back to the pot, and bring it to a boil. Pasta and chopped mint are included. Season with salt and white pepper to taste. Heat before the al dente pasta is cooked.

4. Stir in the lemon juice and chicken julienne, and remove from the heat. Ladle it into soup plates and cover it with lemon and mint leaf pieces.

6. Creamy Italian White Bean Soup

(Ready in 50 Minutes, Serve 4, Difficulty: Normal)

Nutrition per Serving:

Calories 124, Protein 12 g, Carbohydrates 38.1 g, Fat 4.9 g, Cholesterol 2.4mg, Sodium 1014.4mg.

Ingredients:

- 1 tablespoon of vegetable oil

- 1 onion, chopped

- 1 stalk of celery, chopped

- 1 clove of garlic, minced

- 2(16 ounces) cans of white kidney beans, rinsed and drained

- 1(14 ounces) can of chicken broth

- ¼ teaspoon of ground black pepper

- ⅛ teaspoon of dried thyme

- 2 cups of water

- 1 bunch of fresh spinach, rinsed and thinly sliced

- 1 tablespoon of lemon juice.

Instructions:

1. Heat the oil in a large saucepan. In olive oil, fry the onion and celery for 5-8 minutes or until tender. Add

the garlic and fry, constantly stirring, for 30 seconds. Add the rice, chicken broth, pepper, thyme, and 2 cups of water and blend well. Bring to a boil, reduce the heat and cook for 15 minutes, then simmer.

2. Remove 2 cups of the bean and vegetable mixture from the soup with a slotted spoon and set it aside.

3. Combine remaining soup in small batches in the blender at low speed until smooth (it helps remove the centerpiece of the blender cover to allow steam to escape.) Until blended, pour soup back into the stockpot and mix in the reserved beans.

4. Bring it to a boil, stirring regularly. Add the spinach and simmer for 1 minute or until the spinach wilts. Remove from heat and serve on top of fresh grated parmesan cheese. Stir in lemon juice.

Chapter 6: Vegan Recipes

In this chapter we are going to give you some delicious and mouthwatering recipes on Octavia Vegan recipes.

1. Hot Tomato Sauce

(Ready in 30 Minutes, Serve 6, Difficulty: Normal)

Nutrition per Serving:

Calories 228, Protein 10.8 g, Carbohydrates 52.4 g, Fat 2.9 g, Cholesterol 67.2mg, Sodium 369.6mg.

Ingredients:

- 8 ounces of dry pasta

- 1 fresh red Chile pepper, chopped

- 1 red bell pepper, chopped

- 1 onion, chopped

- 1(28 ounces) can of diced tomatoes with juice

- 2 tablespoons of tomato puree

- 2 teaspoons of chili powder

Instructions:

1. Preheat the oven to 300 degrees Fahrenheit (150 degrees Celsius). To a simmer, put a big pot of lightly salted water. Cook for 8-10 minutes or until al dente, drain and add spaghetti.

2. Meanwhile, sauté the chili pepper, bell pepper, and onion in a broad skillet until tender. Add the onions, chili powder, and puree, and simmer for another 2 minutes. For a creamy sauce, puree with a hand blender, or puree in lots in a food processor.

3. In a 9 x13-inch baking dish, mix the pasta and sauce and bake for 15 minutes. Serve warm.

2. Vegetarian Black Bean Burgers

(Ready in 20 Minutes, Serve 6, Difficulty: Normal)

Nutrition per Serving:

Calories 128, Protein 12.2 g, Carbohydrates 56 g, Fat 1.5 g, Cholesterol 0mg, Sodium 615.8mg.

Ingredients:

- 2(15 ounces) cans of black beans

- 1 onion, diced

- 1 teaspoon of water, or as needed

- 2 cups of cooked brown rice

- ½ cup of corn

- ½ cup of cornmeal

- ¼ cup of salsa

- 2 teaspoons of garlic powder

- 2 teaspoons of ground cumin

- ½ teaspoon of chili powder

Instructions:

1. In a bowl, put the black beans and mash them to a smooth consistency.

2. The oven should be preheated to 350 degrees Fahrenheit (176 degrees Celsius). Line the parchment paper with a baking sheet.

3. Cook the onion in a skillet over medium heat for around 5 minutes, until translucent. To avoid sticking, add water if needed. Transfer the black beans to a bowl.

4. Stir in the bean mixture with the cooked rice, maize, cornmeal, salsa, garlic powder, and chili powder. Mix until uniformly mixed, using clean hands. Roll the mixture into eight balls of the same size and shape the balls into patties. Move the patties to the baking sheet and cool until they are ready to bake.

5. Bake the burgers for 15 minutes on a paper-lined parchment baking sheet. Flip and bake until heated and browned, around an extra 15 minutes.

3. Pineapple, Black Beans, and Couscous

(Ready in 25 Minutes, Serve 2, Difficulty: Easy)

Nutrition per Serving:

Calories 227, Protein 24.7 g 5, Carbohydrates 141.2 g, Fat 1.3 g, Cholesterol 0mg, Sodium 1485.6mg.

Ingredients:

- ½ cup of water

- 1(15 ounces) can of pineapple chunks, drained (juice reserved)

- 1 cup of couscous

- 1(15 ounces) can of black beans, rinsed and drained

- ⅓ cup of warm water

- 2 tablespoons of taco seasoning mix

Instructions:

1. In a saucepan, mix ½ cup water and reserved pineapple juice over medium-low heat, bring to a boil and extract immediately from the heat. Stir couscous into the coating solvent. Put aside until the liquid is consumed and the couscous is soft, and fluff with a fork for about 5 minutes. Divide it into 2 dishes.

2. In a pan, whisk together the pineapple chunks and black beans over medium heat. In a shallow bowl, mix 1/3 cup of warm water and taco seasoning mix and pour over the black beans mixture. Cook and stir the mixture for 5-7 minutes, until hot. Couscous spoon to serve.

4. Nutritious and Delicious Pasta

(Ready in 40 Minutes, Serve 6, Difficulty: Normal)

Nutrition per Serving:

Calories 216, Protein 5.9 g, Carbohydrates 29.1 g, Fat 1 g, Cholesterol 27.3mg, Sodium 29.2mg.

Ingredients:

- 8 ounces of pasta

- 3 onions, minced

- 8 fresh mushrooms, sliced

- 1 teaspoon of onion powder

- 1 teaspoon of garlic powder

- 1(5.5 ounces) can of low-sodium, tomato-vegetable juice cocktail

- ½ cup of port wine

- 1 teaspoon of dried oregano

- 1 bay leaf

- 1 teaspoon of arrowroot powder

- 1 cup of water

Instructions:

1. In a large pot of hot, salted water, cook the pasta until al dente. Drain thoroughly.

2. Meanwhile, sauté the mushrooms and onions in ½ cup of water in a large saucepan. Garlic, onion powder, port wine, tomato juice, oregano, and basil are added. Add slowly to the saucepan after first dissolving the arrowroot in a bowl of ½ cup of water, stirring constantly. Within a minute, thickening can occur.

3. To the large saucepan, add the cooked and drained pasta and stir. Put the lid on, then serve warm for 3 minutes,

5. Vegan "Shrimp" Ceviche

(Ready in 45 Minutes, Serve 6, Difficulty: Normal)

Nutrition per Serving:

Calories 116, Protein 1.5 g, Carbohydrates 15.4 g, Fat 0.3 g, Cholesterol 0mg, Sodium 166.9mg.

Ingredients:

- 453 g of carrots, peeled and grated

- 1 cup of chopped onion

- 1 cup of chopped fresh cilantro

- 1 serrano pepper, seeded and chopped

- 3 limes, juiced

- 3 tablespoons of ketchup

- Salt, to taste

Instructions:

1. In a glass bowl, combine the carrots, onion, cilantro, and serrano pepper.

2. Stir in the ketchup and lime juice. Put aside for 30 minutes and season with salt.

6. Quick Vegan Sushi

(Ready in 50 Minutes, Serve 4, Difficulty: Normal)

Nutrition per Serving:

Calories 129, Protein 7.1 g, Carbohydrates 62.8 g 2, Fat 2.1 g, Cholesterol 0mg, Sodium 50.9mg.

Ingredients:

- Make-at-home sushi that is quick, easy, and vegan. Serve with wasabi and soy sauce.

- 1(7.4 ounces) package of precooked brown rice

- 2 sheets nori (dry seaweed)

- 1 bamboo mat

- 1 cucumber, sliced into thin strips

- 1 carrot, sliced into thin strips

Instructions:

1. In a microwave-safe bowl, put the cooked rice and partially cover it. Microwave on high, around 1 minute, before hot.

2. Place 1 nori sheet on a bamboo mat. Using a little water on your hands or a spoon to prevent the rice from sticking. Spread ½ of the rice equally on the nori mat. On the top ½ of the rice, put ½ of the cucumber and carrot slices, and roll nori sheet around rice and veggies using the bamboo mat to help. With the remaining nori sheets and vegetables, repeat.

3. Break each roll into six small pieces and place them in the refrigerator for about 20 minutes to cool.

Chapter 7: Meat Dishes

In this chapter, we are going to give you some delicious and mouthwatering recipes on Lean & Green Meat Dishes recipes.

1. Barbacoa Meat

(Ready in 4 Hours 20 Minutes, Serve 12, and Difficulty: Normal)

Nutrition per Serving:

Calories 316, Protein 18.2 g, Carbohydrates 1.3 g, Fat 26.2 g, Cholesterol 80mg, Sodium 77.3mg.

Ingredients:

- 1360 g of beef cheek meat

- 1 tablespoon of olive oil

- ¼ cup of salt

- 2 teaspoons of ground cumin

- Ground black pepper, to taste

- 2 cups of water, or more as needed

- ½ yellow onion halved and thickly sliced

- 3 cloves of garlic, chopped

Instructions:

1. Use olive oil to cover beef cheek meat. Rub the beef with garlic, and pepper. Cover the beef in aluminum foil and refrigerate until midnight, for 4 hours.

2. Pour water into a slow cooker

3. Arrange the onion and the garlic in the aluminum foil around the beef cheek meat.

4. Wrap the foil securely around the vegetables and beef. In the slow cooker, put the second sheet of aluminum foil over the meat mixture, covering securely.

5. Cook on medium, if it has evaporated, adding more water until the meat is very tender, 7 to 8 hours. Remove foil packet from slow cooker and shred meat using 2 forks.

2. Carnitas-Pressure Cooker

(Ready in 1 Hour and 35 Minutes, Serve 24, Difficulty: Hard)

Nutrition per Serving:

Calories 154, Protein 11.8 g, Carbohydrates 2.4 g, Fat 10.6 g, Cholesterol 42.7mg, Sodium 470.8mg.

Ingredients:

- 1(3721 g) pork butt roast

- 1 ½ tablespoon of salt

- 1 tablespoon of dried oregano

- 2 teaspoons of ground cumin

- 1 teaspoon of ground black pepper

- ½ teaspoon of Chile powder

- ½ teaspoon of paprika

- 2 tablespoons of olive oil, or more to taste

- 1 cup of orange juice

- 1 onion, coarsely chopped

- 4 cloves of garlic, diced, or more to taste

Instructions:

1. Remove the extra fat from the butt of the pig, cut the pork into 2-inch cubes, and pass it to a bowl.

2. In a bowl, combine the cinnamon, oregano, black pepper, chili powder, and paprika. Rub cubes of pork with a combination of spices. Lightly brush the seasoned pork cubes in olive oil and put them in the pressure cooker. Combine the orange juice, cabbage, and garlic to coat the pork cubes.

3. Place the lid on the pressure cooker and secure it, put it over medium heat to full pressure until the pork is no longer pink in the center, around 60 minutes. Let the pressure drop for around 15 minutes, naturally.

4. Take the pork and shredded beef from the pressure cooker.

3. Pork Carnitas

(Ready in 6 Hours and 15 Minutes, Serve 12, and Difficulty: Hard)

Nutrition per Serving:

Calories 250, Protein 16.2 g, Carbohydrates 2.3 g, Fat 19.1 g, Cholesterol 62.5mg, Sodium 2072.3mg.

Ingredients:

- ¼ cup of vegetable oil

- 1814 g of pork shoulder, cut into several large pieces

- 3 tablespoons of kosher salt

- 1 onion, chopped

- 1 clove of garlic, crushed

- 3 tablespoons of lime juice

- 1 tablespoon of chili powder

- ½ teaspoon of dried oregano

- ½ teaspoon of ground cumin

- 4(14.5 ounces) cans of chicken broth

Instructions:

1. Heat the vegetable oil over high heat in a big Dutch oven. Season with salt on the pork shoulder, then place the pork in the Dutch oven. Cook for about 10 minutes, until browned on all sides.

2. Put in the onion, garlic, chili powder, lime juice, and oregano. Pour the chicken broth into the mixture and get it to a boil. Reduce the heat to medium-low, cover, and cook for around 2 ½ hours until the pork is very tender.

3. The oven should be preheated to 400 degrees Fahrenheit (204 degrees Celsius).

4. Transfer the pork shoulder, reserving the cooking liquid, to a large baking dish. Drizzle the reserved cooking liquid with a minimal amount and season gently with salt.

5. In the preheated oven, bake the pork until browned, about 30 minutes. Drizzle the meat every 10 minutes

with some of the cooking liquid, then use 2 forks to shred the meat as it browns.

4. Old Italian Meat Sauce

(Ready in 4 Hours and 30 Minutes, Serve 20, and Difficulty: Normal)

Nutrition per Serving:

Calories 296, Protein 15.2 g 3, Carbohydrates 15.9 g, Fat 16.8 g, Cholesterol 50.8mg, Sodium 788.1mg.

Ingredients:

- 907 g of lean ground beef

- 453 g of ground pork

- 2 tablespoons of olive oil

- 2 onions, chopped

- 1 clove of garlic, crushed

- 3 cups of red wine

- 907 g of fresh mushrooms, sliced

- ¼ teaspoon of dried rosemary

- 4 tablespoons of chopped fresh oregano

- ¼ teaspoon of chopped fresh thyme

- 3(29 ounces) cans of tomato sauce

- 1(6 ounces) can of tomato paste

- 2 tablespoons of grated parmesan cheese

Instructions:

1. In a large skillet, set aside the brown beef and pork over medium heat until it is no longer pink.

2. Heat the olive oil in a large skillet over medium heat and sauté the onions and garlic until tender.

3. Add about half a bottle of wine and blend well.

4. To the skillet, add the mushrooms, rosemary, oregano, and thyme and add another ½ cup of wine and sauté until tender.

5. Add to the mixture the browned beef, tomato sauce, and tomato paste, boil for 1 hour, and add the remaining 2 cups of wine.

6. Simmer sauce over low heat for 2-3 hours, stirring regularly, then serve.

5. Spaghetti Squash with Paleo Meat Sauce

(Ready in 1 Hour and 10 Minutes, Serve 8, Difficulty: Normal)

Nutrition per Serving:

Calories 388, Protein 17 g, Carbohydrates 14.5 g, Fat 29.9 g, Cholesterol 52.2mg, Sodium 167.1mg.

Ingredients:

- ¼ cup of water

- 1 spaghetti squash, halved lengthwise and seeded

- 680 g of ground beef

- 1 white onion, diced

- 1 tablespoon of extra-virgin olive oil

- 1 cup of sliced mushrooms

- 1 zucchini, diced

- 1 green bell pepper, chopped

- 1 red bell pepper, chopped

- 1(14.5 ounces) can of crushed tomatoes

- 1(8 ounces) can of crushed tomatoes

- ¼ cup of chopped fresh basil, or to taste

- ¼ cup of chopped fresh oregano, or to taste

- ¼ cup of chopped fresh thyme, or to taste

- 1 tablespoon of red pepper flakes, or to taste

- ½ cup of extra-virgin olive oil, divided

Instructions:

1. Preheat the oven to 400 degrees Fahrenheit (204 degrees Celsius).

2. Onto a baking bowl, add water. Place the squash halves in the baking dish with the cut sides down, roast for 30-40 minutes until tender.

3. Cook and mix the ground beef and onions in a skillet over medium-high heat while the squash is frying, until the beef is crumbly, evenly browned, and no longer pink. Drain some extra grease and discard it. Set aside the beef.

4. Heat 1 tablespoon of olive oil in a medium-hot saucepan, cook and stir in the mushrooms, zucchini, green and red bell peppers, crushed tomatoes, basil, oregano, and thyme.

5. Simmer over medium heat for about 10 minutes, until the vegetables are cooked and tender. Add the ground beef and onions and stir until mixed. Simmer over low heat, stirring regularly, and finish the spaghetti squash preparation.

6. Scrape the hot spaghetti squash halves inside with a fork to shred the squash into strands and divide it into eight plates. Drizzle 1 tablespoon extra-virgin olive oil with each serving of spaghetti squash and top each serving with a generous amount of meat sauce.

6. BBQ Pork for Sandwiches

(Ready in 4 Hours and 45 Minutes, Serve 12, and Difficulty: Hard)

Nutrition per Serving:

Calories 355, Protein 30.2 g, Carbohydrates 15.2 g, Fat 18.1 g, Cholesterol 82.9mg, Sodium 623.2mg.

Ingredients:

- 1(14 ounces) can of beef broth

- 1360 g of boneless pork ribs

- 1(18 ounces) bottle of barbeque sauce

Instructions:

1. Pour in a slow cooker can of beef broth, and add boneless pork ribs. Cook for 4 hours on high heat or until the meat shreds quickly.

2. Take the beef away and shred it with two forks. It won't seem to work right away, but it will.

3. Preheat the oven to 350 degrees Fahrenheit (176 degrees Celsius). In a Dutch oven or iron pan, pass the shredded pork and whisk in the barbeque sauce.

4. Bake for 30 minutes in a preheated oven or until thoroughly heated.

Chapter 8: Salad Recipes

In this chapter we are going to give you some delicious and mouthwatering recipes on Lean & Green Salad recipes.

1. Easy Caramel Apple Salad

(Ready in 40 Minutes, Serve 12, Difficulty: Normal)

Nutrition per Serving:

Calories 181, Protein 3.2 g, Carbohydrates 20 g, Fat 10.8 g, Cholesterol 0mg, Sodium 227.7mg.

Ingredients:

- 1(8 ounces) container of frozen whipped topping, thawed

- 1(8 ounces) can of crushed pineapple

- 1(3-4 ounces) package of instant butterscotch pudding mix

- 2 cups of chopped apples

- 1 cup of skinless peanuts

Instructions:

1. In a bowl, mix the whipped cream, pineapple, and butterscotch pudding until creamy. In a pudding mixture, fold the apples and peanuts until the salad is well combined.

2. Refrigerate the salad for at least 30 minutes, until fully chilled.

2. Orange, Fig, and Gorgonzola Salad

(Ready in 40 Minutes, Serve 4, Difficulty: Normal)

Nutrition per Serving:

Calories 141, Protein 6.8 g, Carbohydrates 14.6 g, Fat 6.6 g, Cholesterol 22.5mg, Sodium 468.1mg.

Ingredients:

- 2 heads of romaine lettuce, chopped

- 2 oranges, peeled, pith removed, and cut into segments

- ½ cup of crumbled Gorgonzola cheese

- 2 fresh figs, cut into 1-inch cubes

- ¼ cup of vinaigrette dressing, or to taste

Instructions:

1. In a large bowl, combine the spinach, grapes, Gorgonzola cheese, and figs.

2. Drizzle the dressing over the salad and coat it with a toss.

3. Autumn Apple Salad II

(Ready in 40 Minutes, Serve 4, Difficulty: Normal)

Nutrition per Serving:

Calories 202, Protein 5.1 g, Carbohydrates 38.9 g, Fat 4.1 g, Cholesterol 2.8mg, Sodium 40.8mg.

Ingredients:

- 4 tart of green apples, cored and chopped

- ¼ cup of toasted, blanched slivered almonds

- ¼ cup of dried cranberries

- ¼ cup of chopped dried cherries

- 1(8 ounces) container of vanilla yogurt

Instructions:

1. Stir the strawberries, nuts, cranberries, cherries, and yogurt together in a medium bowl.

2. Until uniformly coated.

4. Cranberry FluffErrore. Il segnalibro non è definito.

(Ready in 40 Minutes, Serve 4, Difficulty: Normal)

Nutrition per Serving:

Calories 275, Protein 1.7 g, Carbohydrates 45 g, Fat 10.4 g, Cholesterol 20.4mg, Sodium 103mg.

Ingredients:

- 3 cups of miniature marshmallows

- 2 cups of ground cranberries

- ¾ cup of white sugar

- 2 cups of diced apple

- ½ cup of seedless grapes, halved

- ½ cup of chopped walnuts (optional)

- ¼ teaspoon of salt

- ½ cup of heavy whipping cream

Instructions:

1. Stir together the marshmallows, cranberries, and sugar over low heat in a saucepan, cook and stir until the marshmallows are fully melted, for about 15 minutes.

2. Transfer the marshmallow mixture to a bowl and leave to refrigerate overnight for 4 hours.

3. Stir in the marshmallow blend of apples, oranges, walnuts, and salt.

4. Using an electric mixer to beat whipping cream in a chilled bowl until stiff peaks develop, fold into the marshmallow mixture.

5. Crisp Apples with Citrus Dressing

(Ready in 40 Minutes, Serve 1, Difficulty: Normal)

Nutrition per Serving:

Calories 258, Protein 1.4 g, Carbohydrates 33.6 g, Fat 14.4 g, Cholesterol 11.6mg, Sodium 88.3mg.

Ingredients:

- 1 apple, cored and cut into chunks

- 2 tangerines, juiced, divided

- 1 tablespoon of sour cream

- 1 tablespoon mayonnaise

- 1 teaspoon of white sugar, or more to taste

- 1 pinch of salt

Instructions:

1. In a bowl, mix the apple chunks with 2 teaspoons of tangerine juice. In a cup, mix the remaining tangerine juice, sour cream, mayonnaise, sugar, and spice until the salt and sugar dissolve.

2. Pour over the apple dressing and toss.

6. Jicama, Carrot, and Green Apple Slaw

(Ready in 40 Minutes, Serve 8, Difficulty: Normal)

Nutrition per Serving:

Calories 98, Protein 1.2 g, Carbohydrates 16.8 g, Fat 3.6 g, Cholesterol 0mg, Sodium 63.9mg.

Ingredients:

- 2 cups of shredded Napa cabbage

- 1(453 g) jicama, peeled and shredded

- 2 cups of shredded daikon radish

- 2 Granny Smith apples, peeled, cored, and shredded

- 2 large carrots, shredded

- 1 firm pear, shredded

- ¼ cup of finely chopped cilantro

- 2 tablespoons of olive oil

- 3 tablespoons of orange juice

- 1 tablespoon of lime juice

- Sea salt and pepper, to taste

Instructions:

1. Place the cabbage, jicama, radish, apple, carrot, pear, and cilantro into a mixing bowl. Sprinkle with olive oil, orange juice, lime juice, salt, and pepper.

2. Toss until evenly blended and serve.

Chapter 9: Dessert Recipes

In this chapter, we are going to give you some delicious and mouthwatering recipes

On Lean & Green Dessert recipes.

1. Lime Jell-O® Waldorf salad

(Ready in 4 Hours and 15 Minutes, Serve 12, and Difficulty: Easy)

Nutrition per Serving:

Calories 163, Protein 3.3 g, Carbohydrates 29.3 g, Fat 4.9 g, Cholesterol 0mg, Sodium 115.8mg.

Ingredients:

- 2(3 ounces) packages of lime-flavored gelatin mix (such as Jell-O®)

- 2 cups of boiling water

- 2 cups of cold water

- 4 red apples, chopped

- 4 stalks of celery, chopped

- ½ cup of chopped walnuts, or to taste (Optional)

Instructions:

1. In a bowl of hot water, melt the lime gelatin, and add the gelatin's cold water. Pour gelatin into a mold.

2. Mix the grapes, celery, and walnuts into the gelatin. Cool until it's firm, about four hours. Dip the mold in hot water to remove the salad, put a plate on top of the mold and invert it to release the molded salad.

2. Quick Ice Cream

(Ready in 8 hours, Serve 8, Difficulty: Normal)

Nutrition per Serving:

Calories 73, Protein 0.6 g, Carbohydrates 15.1 g, Fat 0.1 g, Cholesterol 0.6mg.

Ingredients:

- ¾ cup of prepared fat-free vanilla pudding

- 1(8 ounces) container of fat-free frozen whipped topping, thawed

Instructions:

1. For the whipped icing, fold the pudding together.

2. Return to the whipped topping tub and freeze with a partially open lid for 8 hours or overnight.

3. Fizzy Gelatin Salad

(Ready in 5 Hours and 10 Minutes, Serve 6, and Difficulty: Normal)

Nutrition per Serving:

Calories 83, Protein 1.3 g, Carbohydrates 20.2 g, Fat 0 g, Cholesterol 0mg, Sodium 69.4mg.

Ingredients:

- 1 cup unsweetened applesauce

- 1(3 ounces) package of lime-flavored Jell-O® Mix

- 1 cup of ginger ale

Instructions:

1. In a small saucepan, pour the applesauce, and bring to a boil. Add gelatin when absorbed, then set aside for around 1 hour to cool.

2. Whisk gradually in the ginger ale until cooled. Until set, refrigerate for about 4 hours.

4. Applesauce Cinnamon Gelatin Salad

(Ready in 3 Hours and 10 Minutes, Serve 6, and Difficulty: Hard)

Nutrition per Serving:

Calories 124, Protein 1.4 g, Carbohydrates 30.6 g, Fat 0 g, Cholesterol 0mg, Sodium 82.1mg.

Ingredients:

- ⅓ cup of cinnamon red-hot candies

- 1 ½ cups of boiling water

- 1(3 ounces) package of lemon-flavored Jell-O® Mix

- 1 ½ cups of applesauce

Instructions:

1. In a large bowl, melt the candy in hot water.

2. Using gelatin and whisk until dissolved.

3. Stir in a couple of applesauce and ice cubes and chill for 3 hours or until set. And the ice cream, the cold serving.

Conclusion

A healthier, fitter, and happier life involves the acquisition of healthy eating habits and the inclusion of regular physical activity. These habits will in turn promote sustained weight loss in order to ensure that lost weight is not regained over time. It goes without saying that achieving an improvement in health and maintaining the lost weight will proportionally improve all aspects of your life.

The Lean and Green diet is a low-carbohydrate, low-calorie diet that will help you lose weight, as well as improve your health in terms of controlling and preventing weight-related diseases. However, it is important to note that you should not overdo it in reducing carbohydrate intake, because some diets of this type, especially those with very few carbohydrates cause some symptoms or side effects such as: headache, weakness, muscle cramps, fatigue, bad breath, constipation, diarrhea, among others, so if you feel these symptoms, you should consider a modification or variation of the diet, with the help of a health coach or nutrition professional.

On the other hand, the reduction of calories and carbohydrates is not the only cause of weight loss, since in a reduced carbohydrate diet, people may feel fuller or satisfied, by including in their diet a greater amount of protein, green vegetables and balanced fats, which helps to eat less and avoid cravings.

CPSIA information can be obtained
at www.ICGtesting.com
Printed in the USA
LVHW082052010421
683209LV00004B/404